WHY YOU MUST PLAY the LOTTERY

The GOLDEN TICKET is already yours!

4878523

Table of Content

Table of Content 5

Preface 9

PESSIMISTIC APPROACH 17

The curse of the lottery 19

How to divide the jackpot 20

Here are three reasons you shouldn't buy lottery tickets: 21

1. Your money will almost always go further somewhere else 22

2. The odds are against you — way, way against you ..23

3. Lotteries are more likely to pull money from low-income people 24

POSITIVE APPROACH 29

UK 38

Austria 38

Belgium 39

France 39

Ireland 39

Luxembourg 40

Portugal 40

Spain 41

Switzerland 41

GOVERNMENT AND LOTTERY 45

TIPS TO WIN THE LOTTERY 55

Does it really pay to play? 59

The Lottery Hackers 62

    How did Gerry crack the lotto's code? 63

Can you buy lotto online? 64

    Why to play lotteries online? 65

What lotteries can a non-resident take part in? 67

Who can't take part in a foreign lottery online? 69

THE AUTHOR 73

Preface

When talking about lottery we will find different approaches and depending on how we were raised we will have the conservative one: "Lottery is for losers" or the affirmative one: "Who plays the Lottery deserves to win".

Both may have the truth on their side, but there are some facts that I would like to share with you on this little research about Life and Lottery, starting on these to principles: the negative and the positive.

At the time I'm writing this, I'm in the middle of one of my hugest personal crisis any one of you can imagine, and the solution for this crisis I helped to create myself is collecting about $100,000.00 to pay in debt, and one of the ways I tried to fix it was to play the lottery, first randomly and then taking in account the data published on the Lottery websites, about remaining prizes and chances to win. Sometimes I won, but most of the times I lost, BUT WAIT! I lost the money, and the money comes and goes but I won the experience and the experience is a resource not that easy to earn.

Why did I jump into the Lottery and why am I sharing this experience with you? It is not for you to go and spend the money you don't have in Lottery, nor to reinforce your believes that "lottery is for losers", as you were told by your parents and grandparents, but to try to demonstrate that we live in a Lottery Life, where all of our chances to succeed are based in probabilities the same way the Lottery is structured and in most of the times managed by the State itself.

These probabilities, along with the science made us hit the ovum in our mother's ovaries, and before that make our parents meet and fall in love and bla, bla, bla…

Of course, the probabilities made the magic of making our parents match and have us as a spermatozoon and ovum, and the science explains that the strongest spermatozoon will fertilize the ovum, but this will happens only if the spermatozoon (YOU) moves fast and steady enough to make it happen, the same way you made the way through your siblings, the school, your job and or the society as a whole, combining probabilities, science and movement, and using your brain hemispheres depending on the situation if it was creativity, numbers and logic, humor or your reptile/primitive instinct.

Just take a look around:

The first recorded signs of a lottery are keno slips from the Chinese Han Dynasty between 205 and 187 BC. These lotteries are believed to have helped to finance major government projects like the Great Wall of China. From the Chinese "The Book of Songs" (2nd millennium BC.) comes a reference to a game of chance as "the drawing of wood", which in context appears to describe the drawing of lots. Lotteries in colonial America played a significant part in the financing of both private and public ventures. It has been recorded that more than 200 lotteries were sanctioned between 1744 and 1776, and played a major role in financing roads, libraries, churches, colleges, canals, bridges, etc. In the 1740s, the foundation of Princeton and Columbia Universities was financed by lotteries, as was the University of Pennsylvania by the Academy Lottery in 1755. Benjamin Franklin organized a lottery to raise money to purchase cannon for the defense of Philadelphia.[1]

The visa lottery[2] was established by the Immigration Act of 1990 in an attempt to bring individuals to the U.S. from countries that had been sending few immigrants to the United States in the past. Currently, approximately 50,000 foreign nationals per year are awarded visas based on pure luck to come and live permanently in the United States under the visa lottery program. As Wikipedia[3], on 2019 there were 22 Millions Applicants, from all over the world, 2 millions more the US Florida State population or 3 millions less

---

[1] WIKIPEDIA, Lottery, fetched on 7/22/2019 from: https://en.wikipedia.org/wiki/Lottery

[2] NumbersUSA, What is the Visa Lottery?, PUBLISHED: Mon, MAR 31st 2008 @ 10:49 am EDT, fetched on 7/22/2019 from: https://www.numbersusa.com/content/learn/issues/american-workers/what-visa-lottery.html

[3] WIKIPEDIA, Diversity Immigrant Visa, fetched on 7/22/2019 from: https://en.wikipedia.org/wiki/Diversity_Immigrant_Visa

than the total population of Australia calculated in 25 millions.

Or make a simple query on Google:

lottery based

lottery based **admissions**
lottery based **green card**
lottery based **schools**
lottery based **savings accounts**
lottery based **immigration**
lottery based **apartments**
lottery based **nursing programs in california**
lottery based **consensus**
lottery based **on blockchain**
lottery based **movies**

It looks like there are plenty of processes, which defines people's future that start or depend on Lottery Based decisions...

"If you're healthy, if you don't get sick much, if you don't go to the doctor much or use your health insurance much, you are a genetic lottery winner. It has nothing to do with the way you live, nothing to do with doing the right things. It's just sheer luck, and you are gonna pay for that."

RUSH LIMBAUGH

PESSIMISTIC APPROACH

Google — why don't bet the lottery

lottery **ruined my life documentary**
why **you don t want to win** the lottery
is the lottery **a lie**
lottery **is a ripoff**
lottery **curse**
lottery **horror stories**
should i keep playing the lottery
sad lottery **stories**

We all gonna die! We all gonna die! Of course we all will die some day, but not now! Let's give life a chance to show you how nice it is and how plenty of opportunities is filled for you.

On this chapter I will browse for you most of the reasons, some people claim for not to take the chance of play the Lottery and test your probabilities to buy the Golden Ticket. People which I'm sure already played and won, like JPMorgan CEO Jamie Dimon who historically and publicly hated bitcoin and now JPMorgan is getting ahead of the crypto revolution.[4]

---

[4] Matt Egan, CNN Business, Jamie Dimon hated bitcoin. Now JPMorgan is getting ahead of the crypto revolution, fetched on 7/22/2019 from:

Charles Riley, publishes an article on 2012 at CNN Business, that smashes the Lottery for a lot of reasons:

You are not going to win the lottery. Sure, somebody might cash in that $640 million Mega Millions golden ticket, but odds are, every single reader of this story will come away disappointed. The odds of winning the jackpot are about one in 175 million. Talk about a low probability event!.

"The odds are crazy if you think about it," said Romel Mostafa, a professor at the Ivey School of Business. "Especially the mega lotteries. It's just nuts." (Mega Millions latest - CNN)

Playing the lottery is a massively popular $50-plus billion business. It is the most widespread form of gambling in the country. But it's also an exceedingly bad bet. Research shows that the lottery pays out at one of the lowest rates among commercial gambling games.

---

https://www.cnn.com/2019/02/15/investing/jpmorgan-bitcoin-crypto-jamie-dimon/index.html

The curse of the lottery

In 2009, 42 states had lotteries, with total ticket sales of $52.3 billion, according to the Census Bureau. But prizes added up to only $32.3 billion, while states retained $17.7 billion as revenue. Mega Millions aside, certain states are marginally better than others if you're hoping to score. According to data crunched by Bloomberg, Georgia residents are the biggest "suckers." They spend an average of $471 per year on the lottery, or 1% of their average income, while receiving a payout of 63 cents on the dollar.

Massachusetts residents spend more, but their state lottery also provides bigger returns -- 72 cents per dollar played. States, many of which routinely face budget shortfalls, are happy to get the money. Depending on state law, the revenue raised from lottery sales is used to fund all kinds of government programs, including education. Earmarking the money for popular causes makes the state look great, but as the National Gambling Impact Study Commission said in the late 1990s, it is not necessarily boosting budgets.

"There is reason to doubt if earmarked lottery revenues in fact have the effect of increasing funds available for the specified purpose," the report said.

In other words, the money often acts as a stop-gap replacement, not a supplement.

How to divide the jackpot

Lotteries were once prohibited in the United States, but have spread like wildfire since they were introduced in the 1960s. In each case, state governments have maintained a monopoly over the game. State governments often label lottery proceeds as "profit." But another way to think about the lottery is as a tax. After all, the government is collecting revenue from a population that willingly purchases a product -- like a sales tax. The only difference is that the tax is built into the price of the lottery ticket, instead of tacked on at the end. Another frequent complaint about lotteries is that they act as a regressive tax, as numerous studies have shown that lottery games are disproportionately consumed by the poor.

"The poor tend to spend more as a share of their income," Mostafa said. "And that is sad. These are the people who are cash-strapped."[5]

Riley on his article browse the "why nots", but misses offering a better idea for you to invest or spend your money, which most Banks do, like in this article published by Adrian D. Garcia on 2019 at the website Bankrate: "3 reasons you shouldn't buy lottery tickets", where the author browse the "nots" but offers "alternatives":

Here are three reasons you shouldn't buy lottery tickets:
Your money will almost always go further somewhere else.

The odds are against you — way, way against you.

---

[5] Charles Riley @CNNMoney, Why the lottery is not a good bet, Published: March 30, 2012: 1:04 PM ET, fetched on 7/22/2019 from:
https://money.cnn.com/2012/03/30/news/economy/lottery-bad-bet/index.htm

Lotteries are more likely to pull money from low-income people.

1. Your money will almost always go further somewhere else

Bankrate's survey found that 21 percent of adult Americans buy at least one lottery ticket in a typical week. Let's say each ticket cost $2 — that would add up to roughly $5.5 billion shelled out annually. That kind of money, if collectively donated, could more than cover the annual budget of the American Red Cross — a humanitarian organization that services millions of people — for two years. Forty-six percent of the people who said they bought scratch-offs, Powerball or other lottery tickets in a given week said they spend between $1 and $5, according to the Bankrate survey.

Instead of shelling out $2 every week for a lottery ticket, people who put that money in a piggy bank would be sure to hit a $104 reward by the end of the year. While that's not $1 billion, it's enough for a nice dinner or to pad a savings account. When only 29 percent of Americans have a fully funded emergency fund and 23 percent have no emergency savings, $104 can make a difference.

2. The odds are against you — way, way against you

Slowly adding to your piggy bank each week is not as exciting as hearing your numbers called or scratching your way to an instant prize. But it's a lot less risky. Getting your money back is statistically the best you could hope for with Powerball. And even then, there's only a 3 percent probability — a 1-in-37 chance — you'll do that. Hitting that big prize is even less likely at 1 in 292 million.

Investing in the stock market is not gambling, but it still involves risk. That said, if done smartly it involves far less risk than buying lottery tickets. And it's easier than ever to participate. Robinhood, for example, doesn't require a minimum balance, doesn't charge per stock trade and lets you conduct business right from your phone or tablet.

3. Lotteries are more likely to pull money from low-income people

People in the lowest income bracket were the most likely to buy a lottery ticket during the typical week. The Bankrate survey found 28 percent of respondents who made less than $30,000 said they bought at least one ticket each week. Only 18 percent of those with the highest incomes, earning more than $75,000, only bought tickets during the typical week, the data show. Lower-income people are also more likely to buy multiple lottery tickets, which, as Bloomberg reports, means poorer Americans are largely paying to keep these games running.[6]

When you dissect these three reasons from a Banker, you may find some making money interest behind them, for example: *Your money will almost always go further somewhere else...,* what does Bankers really do with our money once cross their doors into their accounts? Only them know! *The odds are against you — way, way against you.*

---

[6] Adrian D. Garcia, BANKRATE, 3 reasons you shouldn't buy lottery tickets, March 22 2019, fetched on 7/22/2019 from: https://www.bankrate.com/personal-finance/why-you-shouldnt-buy-lottery-tickets/

Jajajaja, of course that the Bank will set the odds to benefit you! And *Lotteries are more likely to pull money from low-income people*. Yeah!, the Banks never, ever take advantage of we the "poor", I rather prefer to use the term: people with low amounts of cash/money, there is not such a poor people.

Remember this: The Global Lottery Market was valued at US$ 1,788.1 Mn in 2018 and is projected to increase significantly at a CAGR[7] of 4.6% from 2019 to 2028[8], this is your money and mine, and there are bunch of actors around seeking to have part of that cake, so the Bank will try to have it and so will the religions proposing you to better donate it to their US Free Tax Industry, using the best of their bible repertory, like this:

---

[7] Compound annual growth rate (CAGR) is a business and investing specific term for the geometric progression ratio that provides a constant rate of return over the time period.

[8] Market Watch, Global Lottery Market To See Incredible Growth at a CAGR of 4.6% During 2019-2028, Published: Jan 13, 2019 9:36 a.m. ET, fetched on 7/22/2019 from:
https://www.marketwatch.com/press-release/global-lottery-market-to-see-incredible-growth-at-a-cagr-of-46-during-2019-2028-2019-01-13

*To win many more people have to lose. Even if I win, somebody loses. I'd rather be involved in a win-win situation.

*The lottery denies the realty of God's sovereignty by promoting and affirming the existence of luck or chance.

*It violates the Golden Rule. (Do unto others as you would have others do unto you – Matthew 7:12)

*It appeals to my lowest motivations – greed, materialism, and selfishness.

*It violates a good work ethic. The lottery promotes getting money for doing no work.[9]

---

[9] Greg Burdine, 18 Reasons Why I Don't Play The Lottery, fetched on 7/22/2019 from: http://gregburdine.com/18-reasons-why-i-dont-play-the-lottery/

"There may be less of a chance of losing all the money you put into a mutual fund than there is of losing all the money you put into lottery tickets, but you're never going to win big in a mutual fund."

ROBERT KIYOSAKI

Positive Approach

The first recorded signs of a lottery are keno slips from the Chinese Han Dynasty between 205 and 187 BC. These lotteries are believed to have helped to finance major government projects like the Great Wall of China. From the Chinese "The Book of Songs" (2nd millennium BC.) comes a reference to a game of chance as "the drawing of wood", which in context appears to describe the drawing of lots. Lotteries in colonial America played a significant part in the financing of both private and public ventures. It has been recorded that more than 200 lotteries were sanctioned between 1744 and 1776, and played a major role in financing roads, libraries, churches, colleges, canals, bridges, etc. In the 1740s, the foundation of Princeton and Columbia Universities was financed by lotteries, as was the University of Pennsylvania by the Academy Lottery in 1755. Benjamin Franklin organized a lottery to raise money to purchase cannon for the defense of Philadelphia.[10]

Kelly Phillips Erb, in her article "Everybody Wins! Lotteries Like Mega Millions Benefit Taxpayers, Seniors, Schools and More" of December 18, 2013 published by Forbes online, states the following:

Unlike most Americans, I didn't play Mega Millions yesterday. The odds of winning were 1 in 259 million. Statistically, I had a 1,000 times better chance of being killed by an asteroid or comet than winning - and let's face it, my lucks run more to the "hit by a comet" kind than winning the lottery anyway.

That didn't stop millions of Americans from buying tickets. The lure? The December 17, 2013, payout worth more than $645 million was the second largest jackpot in history. The winning numbers (8, 14, 17, 20, 39 - and Megaball 7) matched two tickets sold, one in San Jose, California, and one in Atlanta, Georgia.

---

[10] WIKIPEDIA, Lottery, fetched on 7/22/2019 from: https://en.wikipedia.org/wiki/Lottery

Mega Millions was originally called The Big Game. A handful of states (Georgia, Illinois, Maryland, Massachusetts, Michigan and Virginia) participated in the multi-state lottery in 1996. Other states, like New Jersey, found the idea of a multistage lottery appealing and signed on. In 2000, the Big Game jackpot grew to $363 million - and interest in the game picked up. By 2002, New York, Ohio and Washington signed on and the name was changed to Mega Millions. Today, Mega Millions tickets are sold in most states, as well as the District of Columbia and the U.S. Virgin Islands: only Alabama, Alaska, Hawaii, Mississippi, Nevada, Utah and Wyoming - don't participate in the multi-state lottery.

Why have so many states signed on? The same reason Americans snatch up lottery tickets to begin with: money.

Federal and state income taxes are imposed on the winner, whether winnings are taken in a lump sump or as an annuity. Taxes are paid when the money is actually paid out, which means that taxes are paid out at once if the lottery is taken as a lump sum and annually if the lottery is taken as an annuity. And yes, winnings are subject to withholding for federal and state purposes.

Interestingly, three of the seven states that elect not to participate in the Mega Millions also have no individual income tax: Alaska, Nevada and Wyoming.

But what about all of those states that sell tickets and don't produce a winning ticket? They're still winners. While about 50% of ticket sales are paid out in the form of prizes, the remainder is split according to a formula. The formula includes expenses: unlike some other games, Mega Millions duties - and expenses - are split between the states. That means shelling out for public relations, broadcasting, legal work and settlements.

What's left over goes to the states (as well as D.C. and the U.S. Virgin Islands). States divvy up lottery revenue dollars according to their own state budgets.

Twenty seven states spend some of that money for education, including New Jersey. New Jersey depends heavily on lottery dollars. The New Jersey lottery - which includes Mega Millions - is the fourth largest revenue producer for the state. Last year, ticket sales in New Jersey topped $2.7 billion, putting a staggering $950 million in state coffers.

Lottery proceeds in New York also support education. Nearly 15% of the state's total education funding to local school districts comes from lottery ticket sales. And New York sells a lot of lottery tickets: the state touts that it is "North America's largest and most profitable Lottery."

California, which boasts a winner this go round, will win twice. By state law, California lottery dollars are used to supplement funding to public education on all levels from kindergarten through higher education. That has translated, since 1985, to $25 billion for public education.

Georgia, also a winner with this jackpot, uses proceeds to fund specific education programs including tuition grants, scholarships or loans at eligible Georgia colleges, universities, or technical colleges via a HOPE scholarship; pre-kindergarten programs; and capital outlay projects including computer and other technological upgrades for schools, technical institutes, colleges and universities. As a result of funding through the lottery, more than 1.6 million students have been able to attend colleges through Georgia's HOPE scholarship program and more than 1.3 million four-year-olds have attended pre-kindergarten.

In Pennsylvania, lottery dollars - including those from Mega Millions - benefit senior citizen programs; it's the only state in the country that earmarks all lottery dollars specifically for this purpose. Last year, lottery dollars paid for 8.3 million meals served at senior centers and delivered to seniors' homes. According to the Pennsylvania Lottery, on average last year, each day, lottery dollars provided 22,700 hot meals for older residents. Lottery dollars also paid for low-cost prescription drug programs for seniors: on average, lottery dollars helped to provide more than 26,600 prescriptions to older

Pennsylvanians, every day. Lottery dollars also helped fund transit and property tax rebates for seniors in the Commonwealth.

And in Wisconsin, the money is returned to taxpayers. Wisconsin Lottery Director Mike Edmonds says that lottery sales go toward lowering property taxes. By the dollars, it's estimated that about half of all Wisconsin sales will go toward a $100 discount on upcoming property tax bills.

As priorities change, so does funding. Prior to 1997, proceeds from the sales of lottery tickets in Texas were deposited in the general revenue fund. Since 1997, funds have been used to support public education: more than $15 billion has been used for public education since that time. In the last few years, additional dollars have been directed to the Fund for Veterans Assistance.

States also benefit from sales tax boosts. While sales taxes are not imposed on the sales of lottery tickets, they are generally imposed on all of the extras you buy alongside tickets. That might include the cup of coffee and a doughnut you buy *while waiting in line. It might also include gasoline at the convenience store or a pack of cigarettes at the counter while you're checking out - in those cases, the feds win, too, through the imposition of excise taxes on items like gas and tobacco. Convenience stores and other retailers report considerably more business when taxpayers are in a frenzy over a potentially huge jackpot. That translates into more sales of goods - and more revenue for taxing authorities.*

And what if the winning ticket isn't claimed? Putting aside the craziness of not holding on to that ticket (lost tickets are gone forever), if a jackpot prize is not claimed within the requisite state-determined time frame, each state gets back all the money that state contributed to the unclaimed jackpot. That money is distributed according to state rules. In Georgia, for example, a fixed amount of $200,000 is transferred to the Georgia Department of Human Resources for education and treatment programs for problem gambling.

Sales of lottery tickets translate into tax dollars and funding for states across the country - as well as the federal government. Whether depending on dollars paid out from what many consider to be legalized gambling is good policy or not might be a moral question. For now, however, whether you play the lottery or not, chances are that you benefit in some way from the jackpot.[11]

Checking on Europe we found the EuroMillions, a lottery that is played across nine European countries. Draws take place on Tuesday and Friday evenings with a minimum guaranteed jackpot of €17 million, which can roll over up to an impressive €190 million. They have a program called: EuroMillions Good Causes, with the following results by affiliated countries:

---

[11] Kelly Phillips Erb, Everybody Wins! Lotteries Like Mega Millions Benefit Taxpayers, Seniors, Schools and More, Published Dec 18, 2013, 10:35am, fetched on 7/22/2019 from: https://www.forbes.com/sites/kellyphillipserb/2013/12/18/everybody-wins-lotteries-like-mega-millions-benefit-taxpayers-seniors-schools-more/#17c608dc3dc9

UK

In the UK, 28p from every £1 spent on National Lottery games, including EuroMillions, is set aside for good causes. More than £37 billion has been raised since the National Lottery began, with over £30 million per week being added to the Good Causes Fund.

More than half a million awards have been granted to projects across the UK, and the figure keeps rising sharply each year. The funds collected are distributed by a number of bodies, covering four main categories – Sports, Arts, Heritage, and Health Education, Environment and Charitable Causes.

Austria

Österreichische Lotterien, which runs EuroMillions in Austria, has been sponsoring good causes under the motto of 'good for Austria' since 1986. Austria's Olympic and Paralympic Committees have been backed by funds raised through lottery games in Austria. A range of other humanitarian and research projects have also benefited, while money has been raised to help the protection of pandas, lynx and bearded vultures.

Belgium

The Belgian National Lottery is committed to helping various good causes and offers grants and sponsorships to a host of projects. A total of €185.3 million was made available for public service grants in 2016, split between 61.95% for humanitarian and social work, 27.44% for donations to the community, 6.5% for culture, 2.92% for sport and 1.19% for science.

France

Française des Jeux, the French National Lottery, is committed to developing athletes with sponsorship programmes, providing social support through sport and helping disabled people access sports. It achieves these aims through funds from games like EuroMillions, which are distributed by the lottery's foundation. The company also sponsors the Française des Jeux professional cycling team, which was founded in 1997.

Ireland

More than €5 billion has been raised for good causes since the Irish National Lottery began in 1987, and approximately 30% of the funds generated from games such as EuroMillions are donated to worthy projects. The money is distributed across the country, supporting local initiatives and larger organisations such as the CROCUS Centre for people with cancer, the Dyslexia Association and the Asthma Society.

Luxembourg

The net profit on all Luxembourg lottery games, including EuroMillions, is donated to good causes in the fields of health, sport, culture, social issues and the environment. The Nationale Grande-Duchesse Charlotte is responsible for distributing the grants on behalf of the lottery and has awarded almost €220 million to date, with beneficiaries including the Luxembourg Red Cross, the National Cultural Fund.

Portugal

The Portuguese Department of Games runs lotteries such as EuroMillions and donates the majority of net income to government departments who distribute the funds in the areas of health, sport, culture and social issues. Of the money provided for beneficiaries across Portugal and its islands, 28% is pledged to Santa Casa Misericordia de Lisboa, a charity dating from the

15th century which runs hospitals and other health centres, as well as supporting a wide range of other projects.

Spain

Loterias y Apuestas del Estado allocates its profits to an array of good causes devoted to social issues, sport, culture, education and the environment. Some of the charitable organisations to benefit from funds from EuroMillions and other lottery games are the Spanish Association Against Cancer, the Olympic Sports Association and San Ildefonso Primary School.

Switzerland

There are two official lottery operators in Switzerland - Swisslos and Loterie Romande. Swisslos supports national sports programmes such as the Olympic team and youth development in football, whilst also focusing on the German-speaking cantons of Switzerland and Ticino across sectors such as culture, sport, social issues and the environment. Loterie Romande provides support for good causes in the French-speaking cantons, benefiting the areas of sport, social action, *education, health, culture, research, heritage, the environment and tourism.*[12]

---

[12] EUROMILLIONS, EuroMillions Good Causes, fetched on 7/22/2019 from: https://www.euro-millions.com/good-causes

"When I go to Afghanistan, I realize I've been spared, due to a random genetic lottery, by being born to people who had the means to get out. Every time I go to Afghanistan I am haunted by that."

KHALED HOSSEINI

GOVERNMENT AND LOTTERY

Why most of the lotteries around the world are monopolized by the governments?

Again: The Global Lottery Market was valued at US$ 1,788.1 Mn in 2018 and is projected to increase significantly at a CAGR[13] of 4.6% from 2019 to 2028[14], that simple: Money.

Alex Mayyasi, in his article "Why Does the Government Have a Monopoly on Lotteries?", established:

They are available in convenience stores and gas stations around the country: lottery tickets, scratchers... the chance to win a fortune. Or, more often, $3. Like any form of gambling, buying

---

[13] Compound annual growth rate (CAGR) is a business and investing specific term for the geometric progression ratio that provides a constant rate of return over the time period.

[14] Market Watch, Global Lottery Market To See Incredible Growth at a CAGR of 4.6% During 2019-2028, Published: Jan 13, 2019 9:36 a.m. ET, fetched on 7/22/2019 from: https://www.marketwatch.com/press-release/global-lottery-market-to-see-incredible-growth-at-a-cagr-of-46-during-2019-2028-2019-01-13

Why you must Play the Lottery

lottery tickets essentially amounts to throwing money away: The expected value of buying a $1 ticket is around 50 cents. But even if you know the odds, there is something to enjoy. The fantasy of getting rich, the anticipation, the ritual of playing, and the burst of dopamine from even a small win.

The ubiquity of lottery tickets is odd. Unlike slot machines or roulette tables, they are not the preserve of Las Vegas. In fact, Vegas is one of the few places where they can't be found. Nevada is one of 6 states that don't allow lotteries. Even stranger, the states that allow lotteries maintain a monopoly on the practice. Why are the same governments banning and regulating casinos responsible for running a form of gambling worth nearly $80 billion in annual sales in the United States alone?

A little history can help us understand how states ended up embracing one form of gambling even as it disdained of others.

Lotteries can claim a proud American heritage. The company funding the settlement of Jamestown held a lottery -- with permission from *the British Crown -- to finance the venture. Lotteries sponsored by all 13 colonies and popular Americans like George Washington financed public works including the construction of Harvard and Yale, churches, and libraries. (The practice of paying for infrastructure with lotteries has a long history that may date back to the construction of the Great Wall of China.)*

Opposition to Britain's rules about the holding of lotteries fueled anger alongside the taxation without representation mantra, and the Continental Congress tried to finance the revolution with a lottery, although it failed to sell tickets. And early America's opposition to taxes made lotteries a popular option for financing government projects in the the young republic.

Lotteries were not without controversy -- a number failed due to either logistical problems, fraud, or moral opposition by those expected to buy tickets. Nevertheless, lotteries remained a staple fundraising tactic into the 1800s. Religious opposition, fraud, and the social reform movements that took on issues like temperance and educational reform eventually brought gambling and lotteries to heel (social reformers believed the lotteries targeted the poor). In 1878, Louisiana ran the only legal lottery in the United States. In the 1890s, national legislation prevented lotteries that crossed state borders and 35 states constitutionally banned lotteries.

Legal lotteries took place only intermittently (although illegal ones still enjoyed popularity) until the Great Depression and World War II, when the need for cash and stimulus overcame the reduced opposition to gambling and lotteries. In 1964, a referendum by New Hampshire voters legalized a lottery to close a state budget gap and fund the school system. A majority of states eventually followed New Hampshire's example.

It's a testament to the endurance of the opposition to gambling that no privately run lotteries exist. (Although some run lotteries on behalf of state governments.) Given the easy money available, it's a miracle lobbying and/or fraud never managed to legalize the practice for private interests.

Politicians, voters, and other actors have legitimized lotteries by linking them to activities of apple-pie wholesomeness: funding education budgets, building libraries... one law during the Depression selectively allowed bingo at churches as donations dried up.

But there's no getting around the dark aspects of lotteries. For starters, even if lottery profits go toward a specific good like the education budget, permanent lotteries don't really support any one aspect of a state's budget. Funding is fungible, so lottery earnings paying teacher salaries frees up other tax revenue to pay for police pensions, infrastructure, or anything at all.

As alluded to above, one could say that lotteries target the poor, or at least that poverty traps enable them. The poorest and least educated 20% of Americans purchase the "vast majority" of lottery tickets, and one study found that households with incomes less than $12,400 spend an average of 5% of their annual incomes on lotto tickets. "Give your dreams a chance!" the New Jersey lottery admonishes residents.

For this reason, some critics call lotteries a regressive (as opposed to progressive) tax. While the word tax may seem disingenuous for a voluntary act, it's perplexing that the same governments trying to protect poor and uneducated consumers from predatory payday loans and credit card fees run programs whose revenues depend on poor decision making (or ignorance of the odds) by those of little means. Is the extra revenue worth the social cost?

One of the few defenses of the government's monopoly is that lotteries constitute a "natural monopoly." Since a few large jackpots hold much more interest for people than many small ones, the logic goes, the industry is most efficiently run in a limited fashion by just one actor. Powerball, for example, has a minimum advertised jackpot of $40 million as of 2012.

We're not sure that passes the sniff test. Vegas shows no shortage of interest in games of chance of all payoff levels, and lotteries in the United States have weathered the large increase in the number of state-run lotteries by designing games that heighten buyers' involvement and anticipation.

A history of mixed prohibition and support helps explain why governments hold a monopoly over the running of lotteries. But in the end, the right explanation seems to be the simplest one, and the same reason everyone plays the lottery: States need the money and are lured by the prospect of an easy way to get it. Only for the states, unlike for all but a few of their poor residents, it actually works.[15]

---

[15] Alex Mayyasi, PRICEONOMICS, Why Does the Government Have a Monopoly on Lotteries?, fetched on 7/22/2019 from: https://priceonomics.com/why-does-the-government-have-a-monopoly-on/

"My wife said to me: 'If you won the lottery, would you still love me?' I said: 'Of course I would. I'd miss you, but I'd still love you.'"

FRANK CARSON

Tips to win the Lottery

Come and take a look at Vanessa McGrady article published in 2016 at Forbes online:

I defy you to find anyone who has never fantasized about winning the lottery. The house! The travel! The help for loved ones and favorite charities! Someone to deliver a single, perfect piece of chocolate to your door every day! (OK, maybe that's just me.)

While most of us will never see that kind of money dumped in our laps, a select few lottery winners do actually get to realize their fantasy—and on Saturday night, someone could win the largest Powerball lottery ever, $700 million.

One of the "luckiest" people in the nation is Richard Lustig, author of Learn How To Increase Your Chances of Winning the Lottery, who has won seven lottery grand prizes and perfected his strategy though trial and error. "When the lottery came to Florida, I was like everybody else: 'Wow, buy lottery tickets, win a lot of money, retire, buy a big fancy yacht, whatever, blah, blah, blah,'" he said. "Like everybody else, I was running out and buying haphazardly, buying quick picks, I mean buying tickets with no plan, or no method, or whatever. Like everybody else, I was losing all the time."

Then Lustig realized there had to be a way to increase his chances. Every time something worked, he'd write it down. Eventually, he had a "formula" that worked for him and others. His main tips--which don't all follow strict mathematical logic, and have been discounted by some as nonsense--for those playing lotteries are below:

1. **Don't use the "quick-pick"** numbers generated from the store's computer. Even though it seems like every number has an equal amount of "luck," certain number sets are better than others. "Every time you buy a quick pick, you get a different set of numbers; therefore, your odds are always going to be at their worst in that particular game, whatever game you're playing. In

this case, the hype, of course, is all about the Powerball right now," Lustig says.

2. **Go beyond the birthdays.** The spread is important—if you always choose birth month and dates, like most people do, you're relegating yourself to less than half the numbers available, 1 through 31. Equally important about including bigger numbers: "If you pick your own numbers and only play birthdays and anniversaries, you're splitting the pot with 20-40 people. If you spread the numbers out across the whole track, you'll either be the only winner or will split it with only one or two people," Lustig says.

3. **Don't change the numbers.** Once you've determined which numbers are "good," (he recommends a specific way to find these in his book) don't switch them, play them every time. If you buy more than one card, use a different set of numbers. "Remember, a set of numbers wins the grand prize, not individual numbers," Lustig says. He says

it's OK to repeat a number or two, but be sure each group of numbers is mostly different so you increase your odds. (Though, if you're looking at this in a solid math sense, in a fair lottery, every number has the same probability of being drawn.)

4. **Play consistently**. "Never miss a drawing in the game you're playing. Every Saturday, every Wednesday, every week," Lustig says.

5. **Understand the odds,** but know your limits: If you play 100 cards, you'll have a better chance than if you pay just 10—but only play what you can afford to lose. It's not a regular investment, as in an IRA or a stock. "One of the things that I preach to people all the time is budget, budget, budget," Lustig says. "Set a budget of what you're going to spend. Do not get caught up in what's called lottery fever. Don't spend grocery money. Don't spend rent money. Figure out what you can afford to spend. Don't worry about how much Joe Blow

down the street is spending. ... Figure out what your budget is, what you can comfortably afford to spend, and stay within that budget."

Does it really pay to play?

Of course, plenty of financial professionals say it's never worth it to play the lottery. Even though there's a lot to be gained, in general, playing Powerball is still a bad decision because you never get the full jackpot, and chances are you'll be splitting it, says Paul Dreyer, a mathematician for the RAND Corporation (who, for the record, fully disagrees with the logic of Lustig's method).

He broke down the probability this way: "There are pieces to the Powerball lottery, the major cash prize and the smaller prizes for matching some, but not all, of the numbers. When you add up the expected earnings just from the smaller prizes, it comes out to about $0.32 per ticket. That means that for every $2 ticket you play, for a ticket to be 'worth it' in the long term, the expected earnings from the big prize should be at least $1.68.

"The probability of winning the big prize is 1 in 292,201,338. The naive argument would be that once the jackpot gets above $473 million, you should buy a ticket because your expected winnings per ticket is greater than the $2 you spent on the ticket."

He adds that most people would think that playing for the $700 million jackpot is a "no brainer," but there are things to consider:

The $700M is a 30-year annuity. The cash now option is typically 60 to 70% of the jackpot. For the current jackpot it is $428.4M, about 61% of the annuity total.

Taxes eat up nearly half of your winnings: The winner will be doling out 39.6%, for federal taxes, and your state (and possibly city) may take a portion. (California and seven other states don't tax lottery winnings.)

Everyone will be playing. For the sake of an example, if all 320 million people in the United States buy a single random ticket the probability that at least one person wins is about 66.6%. "That 'at least' part is key, though," Dreyer says.

"The probability that exactly one person wins is 36.6%. That means that 45% of the time, if you win, you're splitting the jackpot with at least one other person. ... Presumably, the larger the prize, the more tickets are purchased by people, and the more likely you are to split the prize. It is a nasty spiral."

He adds: "However, I have no desire to be a lottery curmudgeon. If you have $2 available and buying that ticket lets you enjoy a momentary dream of your own private island, consider it a cost of entertainment. That statement is predicated on having the $2 available, which gets to the issue of lottery participants which participate in large numbers but may not have the disposable income to support it, namely the poor."[16]

---

[16] Vanessa McGrady, Forbes, It's Math: Why You Should Never Play the Lottery, published: Jan 8, 2016, 06:45am, fetched on 7/22/2019 from:
https://www.forbes.com/sites/vanessamcgrady/2016/01/08/powerball/#2811b0e27065

The Lottery Hackers

A HUMBLE maths genius and his wife became MILLIONAIRES after he hacked the lottery and reaped the benefits for years.

In 2003, retired Michigan shop owner Gerry Selbee, who has a bachelor's degree and a MBA in mathematics, noticed a flaw in new state's new lottery game.

Family man Gerry, then aged 64, realised in "about four minutes" that the new Winfall's "roll-down" gimmick actually gave favourable odds to the player, prompting him to bulk buy thousands of tickets at a time.

Like other lotto games, if no player guessed the six numbers required for the jackpot, the windfall would roll-over to the next week.

However, in this particular game, if the roll-over exceeded more than $5million then the jackpot would roll down to every single tier of winners - including those who correctly chose two, three, four or five numbers.

Gerry, who is a lifelong puzzle solver, realised that as long as no one guessed the six numbers on roll-down weeks, then a $1 ticket was statistically worth more than $1.

He told the HuffPo: "I just multiplied it out and then I said, 'Hell, you got a positive return here.'"

After losing $50 on his first try, the seasoned mathematician persevered knowing that this was simply bad luck.

On his next two attempts he won $6,300 from $3,600 worth of tickets and $15,700 from $8,000.

He soon told his wife Marge and they, along with their kids and close friends, started up a betting group GS Investment Strategies LLC in the small town of Evart, Michigan.

The group brought hundreds of thousands of tickets every time there was a roll-down week and earned between $7.5million and $8million (£5.8million).

How did Gerry crack the lotto's code?
Gerry targeted 'Winfall' games which had a 'roll-down' gimmick

Like other lottery games, the jackpot rolled over until there was a winner

However, in the Winfall game, when the rollover jackpot exceeded $5million the cash would 'roll-down' to every other tier of winner including those who guessed two and three numbers correctly

Maths genius Gerry realised that if he bought thousands of tickets on roll-down weeks then he was statiscally likely to make a profit

After winning over $20,000 after only three attempts at the system, Gerry and his family began buying hundreds of thousands of tickets

In six years of strategically playing the Winfall games - only betting on roll-down weeks - Gerry's group won around $8million (£5.8million)[17]

Can you buy lotto online?

---

[17] Mark Hodge, The Sun, CRACKING THE CODE Puzzle genius cracks secret code to winning the lottery and becomes a MILLIONAIRE… here's how he did it, published: 2 Mar 2018, 10:03Updated: 2 Mar 2018, 11:12, fetched on 7/22/2019 from: https://www.thesun.co.uk/news/5708863/lottery-trick-winners-lotto-gerald-selbee-code/

Objectively speaking, lottery gambling is the only way to win big quickly and easily; therefore it's high time to plunge into the world of Powerball, MEGA Millions, Oz Lotto, and other big games.

Lottery lovers from all over the world prefer American, Australian and European games. Due to the developed culture of gambling in Western countries, one can grow rich having a good habit of taking part in official lotteries twice or thrice a week. You can spend only a week on getting wealthy; other players are able to win in their very first draw. In addition, these lotteries spread extremely large Jackpots, as well as worthy secondary prizes.

Why to play lotteries online?

Here are the main arguments why it's worth playing American, Australian and European lotteries:

Prize pools of all American and European lottos exceed hundreds of millions of dollars and euros. Even the less massive lotto Jackpot is at least several million dollars. For example, the minimal Jackpot of the fabulous American game Powerball is $ 10.000.000; moreover, there is no limit to the maximum amount of its Jackpot. January 2016, the lottery announced 1.6 billion dollars as the major prize. The ultimate prize was shared between three players.

There are a lot of games of luck in the US and Europe: from scratch cards to draw lotteries. The most popular of them are "match 6 out of 49". Normally, they are held 2-3 times a week. Special (bonus) balls are added to other lotteries to make regular draws more spectacular and unpredictable. Thumbs up to winning odds!

American and European lotteries are perfectly organized: not least because many of them have several prize tiers. It means that even the minimum number of matched balls can make you much richer. For example, the second-tier Powerball prize can reach $ 10.000.000.

Many lotteries have additional options, such as the "Multiplier", which can increase the amount of the secondary winning up to 10 times! Many of the European games also have some nice features like additional balls "Complementario" or "Reintegro" or the possibility to even refund the ticket price.

The drawings are always transparent: at any time, lottery players can watch the game on TV or on the Internet. All the lotteries have official websites, where you can get acquainted with the official lotto results, view the gallery of winners, and contact support and ask a question.

The customer is always right! Since the government acts as the organizer of all American, Spanish, Italian, and English lotteries; their quality, transparency and honesty are monitored to avoid incidents. Such names as Powerball, MEGA Millions, and EuroMillions are always synonymous with quality.

What lotteries can a non-resident take part in?
American: Powerball, MEGA Millions, New Jersey Pick-6, SuperLotto Plus, Lotto Texas, New York Lotto

Canadian: Lotto 6/49, Quebec 49, Lottario

Pan-European: EuroMillions, EuroJackpot

Italian: SuperEnalotto, SuperEnalotto Superstar

Spanish: Bonoloto, El Gordo, La Primitiva, Loteria Nacional

Australian: Powerball Australia, Oz Lotto, Saturday Lotto, Monday & Wednesday Lotto

What are the advantages of buying tickets online?

The borders of countries are erased. You can "visit" Australia and America in one day just by buying both Powerball and Oz Lotto.

To buy a ticket, you don't need to leave your house.

Your lotto agent will upload a scanned copy of your ticket to your personal account before the draw.

You don't need to watch the results; you'll receive a notification of winnings by e-mail.

In most cases, your winnings will be transferred to your bank account or bank card. Otherwise, your lottery agent will pay for your plane ticket to the country where you'll be able to claim the Jackpot.

You can ask the consultant questions in the life chat. You will get answers to all of them!

Who can't take part in a foreign lottery online?

The Terms of Use of any lottery allow only adult players to participate in foreign lotteries. If you are under 18, you can purchase a lottery ticket online. But problems can arise when the prize is ready to be paid out to you: for example, you won't be able to set up a bank account that is required to transfer the winnings. In addition, you will embarrass the lottery organizers, who don't have the authority to pay out winnings to underage players.

If you have doubts that you will be given a visa to the state where the lottery is held (for example, if you have large unpaid debts and legal problems), you better refrain from playing. The fact is that large prizes (not only lotto Jackpots) are paid to the winner only in person.

All other players can buy the best American, Australian and European lotteries online! Choose your winning numbers today and get lucky![18]

---

[18] Paula Amores-Martos, Nail it: advantages of buying lottery tickets online, published: 09 Mar 2018, fetched on 7/22/2019 from: https://www.gobigwin.com/information/tips/nail-it-advantages-of-buying-lottery-tickets-online.html

"Life is a lottery that we've already won. But most people have not cashed in their tickets."

LOUISE L. HAY

The Author

Juan Ramon Rodulfo Moya, **Defined by Nature**: Planet Earth Habitant, Human, Son of Eladio Rodulfo & Briceida Moya, Brother of Gabriela, Gustavo & Katiuska, Father of Gabriel & Sofia; **Defined by the Society**: Venezuelan Citizen (*Human Rights Limited by default*), Friend of many, Enemy of few, Neighbor, Student/Teacher/Student, Worker/Supervisor/Manager/Leader/Worker, Husband of Katty/ Ex-Husband of K/Husband of Yohana; **Defined by the US Immigration System**: Legal Alien; **Studies in classroom**: Master Degree in Human Resources Management, English, Chinese Mandarin; **Studies at the real world**: Human Behavior; **Studies at home**: Webmaster SEO, Graphic Web Apps Design, Internet & Social Media Marketing, Video Production, YouTube Branding, Trading, Import-Exports, Affiliate Marketing, Cooking, Laundry, Home Cleaning; **Work experience**: Public-Private-Entrepreneur Sectors; **Other**

Definitions: Bitcoin Evangelist, Human Rights Peace and Love Advocate. **Author of**: Why Maslow: How to use his theory to stay in Power Forever (EN/SP), Asylum Seekers (EN/SP), Manual for Gorillas: 9 Rules to be the *"Fer-pect"* Dictator (EN/SP)

Social Media profiles:

Twitter/FB/Instagram/VK/Linkedin/Sina Weibo:

@rodulfox

Sorry, I try not to tell, but I got graduated as Army Officer at the, once long time ago respectable, Military Academy of Venezuela, I loved that career and love to serve people and nature, but nowadays is a Shame how a large percentage of my fellow Army Mates became enough responsible of one of the most crude Humanitarian Crisis that Venezuela has ever experienced since the Colonization. After this sad experience which by the time of publishing this book, November 2018 has not reach the end, and knowing the behavior of other Armies from countries like Myanmar, North Korea, China, I truly believe that this kind of Armed Organizations must disappear and/or use their Power to Save

Humans from Poverty instead of Keeping Dictators or themselves in Power over the death corps of their fellow Earth Habitants.

```
THE PROFITS FROM THIS BOOKS (IF ANY)
WILL HELP TO SUPPORT PEOPLE
STRUGGLING TO SURVIVE THE XXI CENTURY
VENEZUELAN HUMANITARIAN CRISIS,
CREATED BY HUMANS DECIDED TO STAY
IN POWER, DESPITE DEATH AND SUFFERING
OF OTHER HUMANS AND BY THE MEANS OF
DESTROYING THE EARTH TO SALE OIL AND
MINERALS TO GUARANTEE THEIR
DICTATORSHIP FOR EVER....
```

www.ingramcontent.com/pod-product-compliance
Lightning Source LLC
Chambersburg PA
CBHW030728180526

45157CB00008BA/3092